Pretty
Things
To Say

A. BEYERLEN & Co., STUTTGART.

poems by
William Taylor Jr.

First edition. Printed in the USA.

Six Ft. Swells Press
www.sixftswellspress.com
www.facebook.com/SixFtSwells
Instagram: sixftswellspress

Editor: Todd Cirillo
www.toddcirillo.com

Book & Cover Design: Julie Valin
www.selftoshelfpublishing.com

Various forms of many of these poems previously appeared in: American Journal of Poetry, Angel's Share, As it Ought to Be, Bare Hands, Be About It, Big Hammer, Cape Rock, Chiron Review, Lummox, Misfit Magazine, Nerve Cowboy, Poetry Bay, Polarity, Rattle, Red Fez, Rusty Truck, Rye Whiskey Review, Sparkle and Blink, and Trailer Park Quarterly.

ISBN: 978-0-9853075-8-5

Contents

If You're Free On Tuesday

There is a joy, or better yet, a genuine satisfaction in reading well-crafted poems. Poems you can tell are thought out, revised and edited with each word placed perfectly on the page. William Taylor Jr. can craft a poem and it shows. This is what separates his writing from the thousands of social media poets those of us in the poetry business encounter each day. Poems that get put up on various blogs, Instagram accounts, Facebook pages, online poetry journals, with no effort at revision, editing or even good storytelling. In fact, William addresses this partly in his brilliant and spot on take of modern poetry in the poem *Unacknowledged Legislatures*, "The poets got a poem accepted and they want you to know about it./ The poets got a poem rejected and they want you to know about it./ The poets are posting their works in progress to all the social media sites,/ counting up the likes and shares like shiny coins."

The poems in **Pretty Things To Say** show a sincere respect and affection for the written word and the best part, is the poems do not come off as academic or challenging. Instead, this collection has the feel of a stagger down Lou Reed's *Dirty Boulevard*, the slow burn of Greg Dulli's *The Killer*, or the dark sensuality of Mark Lanegan's *Come Undone*. These are street poems, people poems, poet's poems of raw openness and bare honesty. They are an exploration of cities, people and the poet himself from the vantage point of cafes, barstools, sidewalks and second story windows. The casualness of the poems do not betray the calculation of the talent.

These poems provoke that rare bottom of the dirty boot, stirring in the soul feeling that move the reader to exclaim "Wow" at the end.

William Taylor Jr. is a master at bringing the reader into the scene with him thereby creating a sense of communion, as all good poetry should. In his poem, *The Mistake*, he offers us an invitation, "If you're free on Tuesday/ we could try and find out/ together" and who could resist an invitation like that?

—Todd Cirillo, poet, editor
11:14pm 2/29/20

This volume is dedicated to Sarah Chavez Shelton
1981-2019

Pretty
Things
To Say

• • • • •

• • • • •

poems by
William Taylor Jr.

A Proclamation of Sorts

Lately it's been harder and harder
to find the words
and in truth I don't really mind
so much
as having something to say eventually
becomes as tiring as everything else
I've reached a point
where I am no longer too proud
to proclaim my emptiness
I figure we all
have to cop to it eventually
and now more than ever
I just want to dissolve
into the pretty sadness of the day
the perfect gray sky
above the lonely apartment buildings
the glittering shards of rain
and all the ghosts of the forgotten
and the pretty waitress arrives at my table
with a beer on the house
and the kindness of her face
breaks something within me
and I want to fall into her arms
and weep into her breast
for everything good
and everything lost
and everything we have become
and then I figure I should drink
my free beer first
just in case it gets weird.

The Fire of Now

Sometimes it feels like there's not much
other than the fact of death
waiting just beneath the flimsy
surface of things,
and the crass dullness of our hours
wearing us down like the ocean.
The poets are useless, having
broken with the music of things,
the day an unfortunate
accident no one will cop to.
You find no solace
in the misty gray sky
or the sad old buildings
propped against it,
still haunted by ghosts
of decent things now gone.
You wander the streets
in the soft rain
looking for that old place
with the perfect jukebox,
but they've torn it down
and replaced it
with another safe space
when all you need
is just a bit of pretty danger.
And then suddenly her face
like a prison break,
her lips like a pardon
from this world and the next,
reminding you that the fire of now

is ever equal
to the smugness of the void.
You are struck
by the bravery of her beauty
in the face
of what remains of things,
and you tell her so.
She laughs and says,
why don't you write
a poem about it,
and you do.

Unacknowledged Legislators

The poets are drunk and they want you to know about it.
The poets are sober and they want you to know about it.
The poets are arguing on Facebook again.
The poets love Charles Bukowski.
The poets got a poem accepted and they want you to
know about it.
The poets got a poem rejected and they want you to
know about it.
The poets are posting their works in progress to all the
social media sites,
counting up the likes and shares like shiny coins.
The poets are telling each other how wonderful they are.
The poets are telling each other how horrible they are.
The poets blacklist the poets they find problematic.
The blacklisted poets blacklist the poets
who blacklisted them in turn.
The poets are reading for five minutes
in their three minute time slot.
The poets are working for social justice.
The poets have have no time for social justice,
they're busy trying to harness the sorrow of the world
with a few perfect lines.
The poets are reporting each other on Twitter.
The poets have a new chapbook and its available now.
The poets have only 3 copies left, so you'd better hurry.
The poets hate Charles Bukowski.
The poets are marching on City Hall,
their pockets stuffed with poems.
The poets aren't getting out of bed for three days
straight.

The poets are flying out to AWP.
The poets are starting a GoFundMe account to help them pay their rent.
The poets are starting a GoFundMe account to help them pay their bills.
The poets are starting a GoFundMe account to help them fly out to AWP.
The poets are 5, 637 words into their novel and they want you to know about it.
The poets are waiting to hear from their agent.
The poets are saints.
The poets are prophets.
The poets are liars.
The poets are arguing on Facebook again.

Pirate's Alley

I'm drinking absinthe at a little table
outside a 200 year old bar in New Orleans,
blocks away from the chaos and noise
of Bourbon St. tourists.
It's midnight in August and 100 degrees.
It's quiet here, everything old and pretty.
A black cat with pale green eyes
sits a few feet away and looks at me
without expectation.
I raise my glass and the sweet
liquid burns my tongue a bit.
I am one with Poe and Baudelaire,
channeling the ghosts of ancient poets
as the bright indifferent moon
hangs above.
Even the man-bunned guy at the bar
with the Bermuda shorts
can't ruin this for me.

The Mistake

You're over there looking
like you've just spent
the last ten years waiting
for someone to forgive you
the mistake of being born,
believing you've failed
at most everything
that matters, and no
one's gonna give you
another try, as the years
snicker and speak
your name in less
than flattering tones.
Honey, that's the way
with the lot of us;
the whole world is broken
and not much good.
The dark night of the soul
is granted permanent residence
and nobody knows how much
time there's left to waste.
If you're free on Tuesday
we could try and find out
together, maybe down on the
corner outside the R Bar
in the glow of all those
distant flames.

The Mountains of China

All I've ever wanted was a quiet place
to try and get a few pretty words down,

maybe a window looking out
upon the world as it
burns and fails.

It's getting late now
but I don't regret
much.

We can't be other than we are.

It gets towards the end and people
they climb the mountains of China,
they jump out of airplanes,
swim with sharks.

They want to do everything they've
never done.

I'd like to read a few more books
and have a few more glasses of wine.

I'll take as many more evenings
with my wife and my cats
and the rain outside

as they're willing to give away.

They can keep the rest of it
for those less fortunate.

Except Paris, maybe.
I've never been.

Her Pain

is hand-me-down,
straight off the rack,

everyone on the block
wearing it in one
color or another,

yet she dreams it
a glimmering coat
fashioned from the fur
of some mythic beast,

slaughtered on a slab of ivory
with a diamond blade.

She walks the city
wrapped within it,
imagining every gaze
fixed upon the spectacle,

rather than some other accident,
or something flashing
on the screen of a phone.

My Aura

I get older, and sometimes the bitterness
settles in when I'm not paying attention,
muddling through the fog of the days,
forgetting to listen to the music of things.

When it gets like this I walk the city
in search of unfamiliar streets and alleyways,
some new place to drink beer in the sun.

I pass old apartment buildings and corner stores,
all full of people I'll never know.

In the barbershops they chat
and read magazines,
they wait in metal chairs
for their turn to come.

I find a comic book store and these days
comic books cost like 5 dollars
instead of 35 cents,
and you buy them in these special stores
instead of 7-11s or gas stations
the way you did back in the day.

The guy at the counter looks the way
comic book guys always have;
shaggy and overweight, a bit
standoffish but ultimately friendly enough.

I buy 27 dollars worth of comics

and continue on my way.

I pass by a fortune teller place
where a pretty girl stands outside.
She tells me I have a good aura
and that she's having a special today
if I'd like to step inside.

I tell her maybe on the way back,
and am momentarily sad
as I reflect upon the fact
that when pretty girls on the sidewalk

beckon you, they most always want
money or a cigarette, or to sell
you something you don't need.

I find a bar that looks okay,
there's a seat by a window
where I can read my comics
and watch the people as they pass.

Halfway through my second beer
I've regained a bit of a feel for things,
and I consider going back
to let the pretty girl
read my aura after all,

as outside this slightly
dirty window

people kiss

and empires fall
just like yesterday
and tomorrow.

Sirens

I wander the city with my tourist's
heart half drunk on fear and desire,

the hollowness of the afternoon
breaking like a dawn
nobody wanted.

An old man on Market Street
plays a violin, the sound of it
giving voice to the ancient
sorrow that surrounds us
like a mist.

A kid on a corner
sells maps to dead stars

as a skinny girl says into a phone,
please don't look for me no more.

People in lines at grocery stores
wave expired coupons
like so many flags
of conquered countries,

while billboards flash and offer
yesterday's machines.

The air is filled
with the songs of sirens

and not the sexy kind
with breasts and soft music
to lure you to your doom,

but the ones that come searching
and screaming for you
when you're already
pretty much there.

Caught Up

I'm at the Lush Lounge
drinking beer and trying
to knock some mediocre
poems into shape
trying to make them sing a bit
in spite of themselves
I'm looking out onto Polk street
and all the stupid people
in their ugly cars
stuck in the traffic
on their way to nowhere good
honking their horns
at people who are honking their horns
at people who are honking their horns
at nothing
sometimes I wonder why
we don't just stop
and do something
other than what we're doing
while there's still time
but we're caught up
in the machination of it all
you can't pause
to think about it
you just have to sit there
stupid in your ugly car
honking and honking
telling yourself
it's what god
or somebody intended.

Florida or Somewhere

If the televisions
and computer screens
can be believed,

the woman killed
yesterday by a hurricane
in Florida or somewhere
else I've never been

was the most
beautiful soul I never
had the chance
to meet,

an honest-to-goodness
angel, all the tearful
faces agreed.

I don't know what
to do with this information,
chopping meat in my kitchen
on a Monday afternoon.

I do wonder a bit
at the fact of so many
of the dead harboring
such glistening souls

while the mess of us
still puttering about

the wretched earth
are less than admirable
on the best of days.

In this afternoon's reports
of sundry victims
of cancer, fires, foreign
wars and hearts that
have finally
given up,

there wasn't a
bully or coward
among them,

no sociopaths,
litterbugs,
or anyone
morally deficient
in the least.

I think of the aging junkie
lady with the crooked
smile who lived
in the building next to mine
until she disappeared
one day

and how they never showed
her photograph on CNN
as a parade of televised
faces testified on her behalf.

I stop looking
at the news and eat my meal
with a bottle of wine.

I turn on the stereo and some crazy
jazz pours through the speakers.

It's a glorious mess of noise
and sounds like the deaths of angels
and junkies and everything
in-between

and I raise my glass
to the truth of it.

The Orbit Room, Bloomington Indiana

Here in this Midwestern college town
everyone is 23 years old and every
other building is a brightly lit
sports bar,

flat-screen televisions
above every urinal.

I am here for strange reasons,
wandering about a Friday night
invisible to the crowds of men
in shorts and backwards baseball caps
and women in sleeveless dresses.

I have the luck
to find a little sign on a sidewalk
with an arrow pointing to a flight
of stairs leading down which I

follow to a dim-lit basement
that turns out to be a bar.
The music is okay and there's
a decent selection of beer.

I sit down to order something
and the fellow on the stool next to mine
shows me card tricks and doesn't ask for money.

He's pretty good and the bartender is kind
and pretty and sways in boredom

to whatever tune is playing.

It's nice to gaze upon her until sleep
takes me back to my little room

and there are so many of you out there
demanding grander victories from life
and I've never understood.

Algorithms

Emerson says poetry
must be its own end
or it is nothing.

The poets look troubled,
wounded from
the Twitter Wars of 2018,

unsure of their brand,
wondering if their content
might be deemed
problematic.

Emerson says the verse must be alive,
inseparable from its contents,

as the soul inspires
and directs the body.

The poets wonder
if maybe the algorithms
are working against them,

worrying they've put stock
in obsolete platforms,

blacklisted the
wrong publications,

chosen questionable fonts.

Emerson says we measure
inspiration by the music,

as the poets walk without rhythm
through tedious neighborhoods,
swiping left like phony gods.

On the Occasion of Lawrence Ferlinghetti's 100th Birthday

At Vesuvio Café just across from City Lights
you can still get a perfect Bloody Mary
and sit at a balcony table with your
tattered notebook and your head
full of useless dreams,
just like them beatniks back in the day.
Down in Kerouac Alley a double-decker bus
dumps a batch of sun-addled tourists
out into the afternoon, and they mill about,
squinting at the signs and the plaques,
until a fellow in a baseball cap says, *Jack Kerouac,*
he was the guy who wrote Catch-22
back in the 1960's. His companions
nod and take pictures with their phones
of what they couldn't say,
until they're herded back onto the machine
like so many heads of poorly-dressed cattle.
Over at Columbus and Broadway
there's a palpable shabbiness to things,
because Carol Doda is dead, and Gregory Corso,
and Richard Brautigan, Mr. Ginsberg,
and so many other folks who
brought a certain magic to the world
just when it was needed.
Now the Salesforce Tower looms
like a cheapass eye of Mordor,
and death weaves through Market St. traffic
like an Uber car they won't let you cancel,
but if you're lucky you've got

another few minutes
until it arrives, and look!
There's ol' Ferlinghetti
shuffling down the avenue
like a lost angel,
like a miracle they forgot to revoke,
and suddenly everything is pretty in the dying light
as the ghosts and the tourists
and the drunks and the bartenders
all clasp hands and chant:
Holy Ferlinghetti! Holy Bloody Mary!
Holy dying San Francisco
in the dying light!
May you be born again forever
as all the hearts break
like promises beneath a perfect
North Beach sun!

Another Poem about Burning

I had a thing
for the artists
from early on.

Writers,
poets,
rock stars,
creators.

I'd read their books
and play their records,
I'd study the way they
held their cigarettes.

I'd sit in my room
with the stereo turned loud
as my parents fought
through the night.

The artists understood
that everything and everyone
was forever on fire,

and the only thing to hope for
was the chance to burn in some way
that nobody else had yet managed
to burn.

I found myself harnessed
with the desire

to commune with the darkness,
to learn its language
and forge it into something
resembling light,

something as pretty
and as useless
as that punk rock song

I'd play again
and again,

even after my dad
banged his fist on the door
and told me to
stop.

Talking About Brunch

I'm drinking dark beer on a downtown
patio on a rainy San Francisco afternoon.

I'm emptied of poetry, and the celebrity
deaths of the day are lackluster.

I've fallen out of love with the city
and most everything else
I can think of.

I've nothing to tell and no one
to tell it to,

just these dreary little people
and their dreary little souls.

They're honking their horns
and looking at their phones.
They're talking about brunch,

missing buses, sharing rides,
digging through garbage
and I can find nothing
else to say about them.

I'm bored of their pain
and crumpled paper hearts,
their neon loneliness

waiting to be forgotten

like last week's shooting
or somebody's name.

The Sigh of the Night Shift Waitress

It's my belief that if you hope
to unearth the grace in any
given moment, you have to
find the music in it.
Even if it's sad, even if it
doesn't have a tune to whistle to,
even if you think it isn't there.
It's necessary to transcribe the noise
of distant traffic on lonely freeways
and the sigh of the night shift waitress
as she pours another weak coffee
for the regular whose name
she's never asked.
You have to find the music
in the sound of someone
not answering the phone at 3 a.m.
as the rain pours down if you ever
hope to sing.

Your Abandoned Joy

Kid, no one's gonna give you
back your abandoned joy,

you gotta steal it
when nobody's looking,

or even when they are,

flipping 'em the bird
like you mean it,

running until you turn
into fire again.

A Seventeen Dollar Glass of Wine and the Early Works of Matisse

I'm drinking overpriced wine
in the café at the Museum
of Modern Art on a Tuesday
afternoon.

Summer is done and the tourists
have gone back to whatever sad places
spawned them.

Everything is quiet and civilized
as I sip the Chardonnay of the day
while reading about Baudelaire
and his miserable genius.

The women are pretty
in skirts and dresses
whispering to each other
as they gaze upon some lesser
work of Edvard Munch.

Everything is clean, white and pristine
while outside are all the things
the headlines drone on about:

cancer and freeway crashes,
things on fire and the inevitable
collapse of every decent
thing we've ever known.

But it all seems so far away
and meaningless when
compared to what Matisse
achieved in his later years

and it feels pointless
to dwell upon such dreariness
when confronted with Warhol's
comic book yellows
and reds.

Here, the mistakes of our past
have been captured and neutralized,
handsomely framed and placed
upon the walls with gilded
plaques of explanation

so that we might see
and soberly contemplate
for a moment or two
before moving on
to something else

and then back downstairs
for another glass of wine
before everything
closes.

Leave Me Alone, I was Only Singing

At some point someone discovered
it is easier to destroy than to create,

and that's how it started.

They went and canceled beauty
because it was problematic
on the best of days,

they exiled it to the wasteland
of unsafe spaces.

They gathered up
the poets
and the artists,

both the living
and the dead,

greeted them
with howls
of execration

before extracting
confessions
and apologies

for the harm
they had done
the communities,

and went on to erase
their works and bodies
in solemn ceremony.

They played a concerto
of whatever semblance
of music was still allowed,

to commemorate the occasion,
to usher in the new golden era

in which all bad dreams were banished,
and every good citizen too woke to sleep.

Nervous Eating

Back when I was a young man
still living at my parents' place
I'd sit up late in the den
watching tv, sipping on something
I'd swiped from the liquor cabinet.

I'd hear my dad shuffle in the kitchen.
He'd open the fridge
and start eating on anything
that didn't need to be cooked
or heated up.

He'd stand there
munching on whatever,
and every now and then
he'd say,

What're you doin', boy?

Watching tv, I'd say,
what're you *doing?*

Nervous eatin',
he'd reply.

It was a phrase my mom used as well,
sighing about the weight she'd gained
from all her nervous eating.

I was never quite sure

what they were always so nervous
about, as more often than not
I wasn't aware of anything
particularly troubling
going on.

Of course now,
some thirty years on,
I understand perfectly well
that they were nervous about

the persistence of time,
unpaid bills,
their useless kids, old age
and sickness unto death,
the future
and the past,
the living and the dead
and any number of other things
that make up an ordinary life.

And I think of my father,
now long gone,
as I stand in the cold
light of the refrigerator,
folding lunch meat
into my mouth
at 1:42 a.m.

Late Sunday at Vesuvio

You eventually reach a point
when time becomes a thing
that chases you
with a flashlight, a mirror,
and a finely bound edition
of your collected failures,

and it finds me again, here at my
balcony table, with that sinking feeling
that I will fail to solve the major
and ongoing problems of existence

before the yoke of Monday morning
pulls me back to the reality of things
like an animal to the mess it's made.

I console myself with the fact
of this glass of wine,
the sun still in the sky,

and imagining there's still time enough
for everything to fall into place,
and everyone to be saved,
forgiven, and redeemed
before the big darkness comes.

I'm watching three guys down in Kerouac Alley
smoking something that makes their heads
shake funny,

as the woman at the table next to mine
declares that right now she is so fucking fucked up,

and me, I'm just trying
to get there, too.

The guys in the alley,
they're jerking their heads
and talking to the dirt

as I pray for the pretty waitress
to hurry and bring me something good.

My Luck

I choose this moment
to recognize and embrace
my luck,

sitting at a sidewalk table
in North Beach
working on my second
glass of wine,

halfheartedly editing
poems and stories

as Marina District girls
drink and talk

about things I thought
people only talked
about in movies.

Most people upon the earth
have never had it
so good,

and the next thing you know
neither will I.

More Ghosts Than I'll Ever Know

I don't have much to tell you about other than
the blanketing sadness of this Sunday afternoon
disintegrating into evening, and how I've never known
how to write about anything other than the eventual
death of myself and everything I've tried to love.
I'm here at the Lush Lounge and there's an old guy
at the bar in full regalia, a survivor of something.
He's looking out the window with a faraway face,
and he's probably forgotten more ghosts than I'll
ever know. A woman at the end of the bar
downs a shot and starts to bark, while another
lady buys the old guy a drink and salutes him
as he pours it down. The barking woman is talking
loud about something I can't figure out.
I'm bored with it all but don't feel like going home.
I look out onto Polk Street at the drunks,
the lost, the girls in yoga wear,
the beautiful and not so beautiful people
standing on corners, smoking
and talking and looking at their phones.
Some old woman stooped in rags
shuffles through the alley scouring
the asphalt for scraps of anything,
and I'm on my second beer,
writing the same fucking poem
over and over, and that's
just the way of things.

The Faces of the Beautiful

It was the first decent rain in a while,
the air and the sidewalks smelled of it.

I walked to the corner
for a sixer of something dark.

Back home I drank and listened
to old records on the evening
of my fiftieth birthday.

A half a century upon the earth!

I felt I should document it somehow,
but had nothing in particular to say.

At some point hope and despair
merge into a soft gray mist,
and hardly anything
is ever as good
or bad as you'd imagined.

Like Hamlet says, the world
is a jumble of shit you don't
feel much like doing,
but mostly seems a better bet
than whatever else
might be waiting.

Love is worn, half busted,
but the beer is good, and the music,

and the sound of the rain.

I've seen and done some things,
more than some, less than most.

I've touched the faces of the beautiful
and wept with a sorrow I didn't
know was there.

I'm older than Albert Camus and Kurt Cobain,
older than Janis Joplin and James Dean.

I'm older than Anne Sexton and Jesus Christ.

Despite the years I'm pretty much
the dumb dreamy kid
I was at sixteen.

At this point there's probably
not much left to happen,
but could be there's still time enough
for a few more decent things.

This is what I think as I
get up to turn the record over.

Sunday Afternoons

We are the not so
beautiful losers

drunk on Sunday afternoons

dismantled
and heart extracted

wandering the city's
sad-pretty streets

singing songs of forgotten poets
to music only ghosts remember

wary of the sun
confused by tourists

frightened of the girls of Union Square

the terrible beauty of their faces
as bright as god

as indifferent
to our prayers.

God's Forgiving Sun

Across the street there's some old guys standing outside
of Gino & Carlo,
they're smoking and wearing baseball caps like
cheap ass crowns. They're telling stories
and laughing at the joke of the world
like they were in on it the whole time.
And there's these other nice people out here drinking
beer at the sidewalk tables, who seem to have made
a peace with things. Two ladies next to me,
about my age, talking and sharing a bottle of wine,
like everything wasn't falling apart around them,
like the air wasn't full of ash,
like evil wasn't winning.
Like it was a perfectly pleasant afternoon
beneath god's forgiving sun.
I curse whatever vanity it is
that keeps me thinking the sufferings of myself
and everything upon the earth
are any of my goddamned business,
but I can never quite let it go.
And now the ladies with the wine
are laughing until they cry,
and I'm over here glowering at my plastic table,
sipping at my beer, wrestling
with the death of everything like some
asshole gladiator destined to lose,
while across the street those old guys in their hats
are lighting up another one and laughing like kings.

The Lines for the Urinals of Hell
(for Joe Pachinko)

There's those people who live life
as if it were some perfectly acceptable state of being,
like the days and hours
were workable, bearable things,
while me and everyone I know and love
wake daily into chaos,
traversing moment to moment
like dizzy clowns on razorwire,
swaying over pits of fire and void,
high above the fucks
who walk seemingly easy upon the earth,
who try and hide their fear
like people couldn't smell it
a mile away or see it
in the movement of their hands,
while we wear it like our Sunday best,
offering up daily sacrifices
of wine and blood
and who knows what,
with a despairing bemusement,
a confused and desperate joy.
In truth, I'm just throwing all these words out here
hoping something will stick.
See, I'm trying to get around to
writing a poem about Joe
and I don't know how.
Joe, he'd stay up for days drinking whiskey
shooting shit and cracking jokes
with the saddest truths this dumbass world could muster.

He knew the absurdity of our hours by name,
made friends with the madness and fire and wore it
like a goofy hat.
They say there's no escape for anybody,
but I think maybe if you have the force of will
to choose your own madness and your own fire,
then maybe that is something,
but that's probably as much bullshit as anything else.
The lines for the urinals of hell are twisting and endless,
but hey Joe I managed to sneak in some shitty wine.

December at the Buddha Bar

I was walking to North Beach for cocktails
and was deep in Chinatown when I decided
I could use a drink first.
I stepped into the Buddha Bar,
a dark little dive of a place
with the Red Hot Chili Peppers on the jukebox
and a genuine Chinese bartender
playing liars dice with a group of tourists
and locals.
I bought an American beer
and sat down at a corner table by the window
where I could look at things and not have to talk.
I listened to the bartender's stories,
the banging of the dice cups upon the bar
and the cigarette laughter of the blonde woman
who was apparently winning.
Outside people were Christmas shopping,
deciding on restaurants,
yelling at their children.
I suppose it was the beer but I found myself
enjoying the feel of it all;
the colors of the buildings,
the holiday lights,
the gray of the sidewalks
beneath streetlamps.
I didn't even mind the people too much.
All darker things seemed toothless and distant;
we were figures in an Edward Hopper painting,
everything momentarily decent
or at least redeemable.

I think I could have stayed there forever
sipping at my beer,
basking in some eternally perfect moment in which
nothing hurt
if it hadn't been for the fucking Red Hot Chili Peppers.

Something

I woke up today
and in the morning
news read about
a popular fashion
designer taking
her own life.

Though I myself
had never
heard of her,

the article
went on to say
how she was
famous, successful
and well-loved.

She was wealthy
and attractive,
a wife
and a mother.

She lived a life
most of us can
only dream of

and she hung herself
with a fashionable
scarf.

I don't know
what it says
about me

or these times
that have found us,

but my first
honest thought
was,

well shit
at least somebody's
doing

something.

Santa Cruz

I started drinking early
because the hotel room was sad

and the seaside town
just another place
that was no longer home.

I'm full of cuts and bruises
from falling into things

and your face soft beneath
red lights in quiet rooms
spoke of every pretty thing
I was careless enough to lose.

In the thrall of such moments
I'm inclined to forgive
the universe and everyone
for the ugliness of things

but there's always some angry
god or other
waiting to cast us out
of any decent place
we try and carve our names upon

and on the train back to the city
hungover with a few hours sleep

I wondered if we'd held

hands in the cab or was it
just something I'd dreamed

but it's not the kind of thing
you ask.

Dearest Friends:

I'm lost again,
scrambling for butts
of grace
in the gutters of the afternoon,
hiding from anything
that's ever known my name.
I'm at the Lush Lounge
where there's beer
and the Kinks playing
on the internet
jukebox thing,
so the world holds
together
for a few minutes more.
And now it's Blondie,
so let's just sit
and drink holding hands
while Heart of Glass
plays forever
and dismiss the darker things
roaming the dirty streets
with our dirty names
in their dirty pockets.
Poets today, they got
t-shirts and podcasts,
they got twitter communities
and micro-blogs,
but hardly any poems
worth mentioning,
so I don't know

where to turn.
But now they're playing
something from
Devo's first record
and that should
get me through
the next line
or two, and
after that I
couldn't say.

The Bevmo Lady Has Gone Insane and I am Out of Wine

Your good intentions for the afternoon
are machines full of unanswered calls,

boxes of unfinished letters forgotten
in the garage or given away.

And the poems, they don't want to be born,
they don't want the trouble of being dragged
into the world anymore than you or I.

They're fine as they are, left alone as the mist
on the fur of the lost dogs asleep in the alley,

unborn in the eyes of the skinny girl in the Greyhound
station clutching a one way ticket to some town
with a name you've never heard.

I go to the Bevmo for wine
and there's an older lady at the counter.

I say older, but she's younger than me.
I put my stuff on the counter and ask how she is.

Crazy, she says.

Okay, I say, and laugh a bit.

I put my card in the thing
and she asks if I want a bag

and I say, *sure.*

I really think I'm losing my mind,

she says to no one in particular
as I step away.

Outside everyone is standing in lines
in front of buildings as if it were
what they were born to do.

The streets are full of people,
animals and objects
I lack the power to save.

Some days the loneliness of things
is the only sun shining,

the only restaurant open,
the only one who shows to the party.

Some days the loneliness of things
is the only song on the jukebox of eternity

and you either have to dance or go home.

Our Blood

And if the beautiful things
that fall from your lips
are only beautiful

for as long as it takes
them to fall from your lips,

that's still more
than was promised.

It's early yet,
the drinks are pretty,

and there's some sexy doom
spilling from the juke.

Our blood,
it remembers how to sing.

And if we're only beautiful
for as long as it takes
the bartender to see fit
to shut us down,

that's still more
than the nameless dead
clutch in their sad
forgotten hands.

The Glory

We're at the Lush Lounge on a Monday afternoon
and I happen to mention to the fellow next to me
how the banality of the average day
holds us like a prison,
and the gentleman spins upon his stool
to face me, shaking a finger at the air, saying,
that is simply the voice of your hubris!
We are alive in a glorious universe
in the midst of a glorious people,
and if you cannot banish
the banality of the day
with your own powers,
the fault is yours, my friend!
Our dooms and demons
are born of our own sorry choices
and attitudes, nothing more!
He spins back around,
leaving me to my silence
in which I drink beer while
considering his worldview,
eventually conceding
some plausible truth to it,
as the the women walking
up Polk Street in their springtime
dresses and yoga pants
surely possess some sort
of otherworldly glow
that well might, in certain circles,
pass for glory.
A man I have christened Dirty Santa

leans through the window asking for change,
reminding me as he does
that he is a Christian soul,
imagining somehow
I am partial to such creatures.
The barmaid shoos him away
and rightly so, blocking, as he was,
my view of the girl standing
across the street in red velvet pants
gloriously smoking a cigarette.
A fellow in a tattered shirt
and shit-stained jeans
looking battered by the glory of things,
drunk with it, really,
is doing some kind of tap dance
through the afternoon traffic
in time to a glorious
music in his head,
until a kid in the back seat
of some obsolete machine
chucks something
that might be a half-eaten burrito
and the thing hits his head
with a glorious squelching thud,
and the man crumples into the street
like a dirty ragdoll,
flailing about as the cars
and things speed by
without slowing, desperate
for their sundry destinations.
I turn to speak again to the man
next to me but he is angrily shouting

into a smart phone the size of a laptop,
red-faced beneath the glow
of the gloriously large flat-screen televisions
as the bartender like some angel asks
one more, and I say please.

The North Beach Festival

It was my intention to be fashionably late
but the whole thing was running behind
so I arrived in time to see the children's musical
production of the lives of Emperor Norton and his dogs.
The kids on the ramshackle stage
seemed confused and couldn't sing very well
and every few minutes the two big speakers
shorted out and exploded with feedback
as the frightened children cowered
with their hands over their ears.
At some point one of the dogs fell off the stage
and what there was of an audience gasped
as the creature hung there in its harness
paddling the air.
The mess of it all lurched awkwardly along
to a lackluster finish and then it was time
for the poets, of which I was one.
The parents of the singing kids
and the owners of the dogs had largely
dispersed and what remained of the audience
were a handful of tourists who had
wandered into the wrong beer garden.
The poets were milling about, waiting
for their turn to perform so they could
get the hell out of there as well.
Much of what followed was the reason
why people don't go to poetry readings.
My turn came and I read my stuff
and a few people laughed at the right places
which I considered victory enough.

I collected my 50 bucks
and found another beer garden that didn't have
any poets and within a few hours
my poetry money was gone;
most of it I drank and the rest I gave
to anyone who asked, because it was
as much theirs as it was mine.
I woke up the next day at two in the afternoon
to the worst hangover I'd had in years.
I sat in the house for a day and a half
with a heavy depression, eating pizza
and playing video games. This morning
I felt a little better and I tried to write
and I tried to paint but nothing came and I felt
certain I would never create or love again
but eventually managed to take a bath and then
got outside and made it to the comic book shop
where I bought the latest issue of the Hulk
which I read in a little bar while drinking beer
wishing I had spent the years creating
something useful like comic books or detective novels
instead of poetry but its too late for that kind of thing
and now I'm typing this poem
watching the people mill about Polk St.
a few of them beautiful most of them not
and I guess it feels as okay as anything.

Until the Ghosts Forget

She's got the loneliness of the world
tattooed upon her heart
like the lyrics of a song.

She stays up and drinks
until the ghosts forget
why they were so angry
and drift back
into the soft of the void.

She opens a bottle and listens
to the noise of the city;

the laughter and the sirens,
the makings of ill-conceived deals,
beginnings and endings of sad affairs;

the music of it all more honest
than any lover she'll ever know.

Peace and Love Forever

I'm sitting in the little bar
on Haight St. near the record store.
I'm having a beer, the Cure
are on the jukebox
and the bartender is nice in a gruff
bartender kind of way.
The girls are pretty in their skirts
and dresses as they walk by with their brand new
Jimi Hendrix record albums.
Life and all its mess feels momentarily reasonable,
while death seems impossible and unnecessary,
even though it's happening always everywhere,
like maybe right now in some little apartment
above the t-shirt store across the street,
next to the wall with the mural of Jerry Garcia
that says peace and love forever,
as the old hippies shuffle by
in their ugly tie-dye shirts
like there's still
a chance for something.

The Dreams of Billboards

And when your time comes,
whether it's five minutes from now
or forty years,
and whether you're letting go your last frail breath
from a sad bed in some old folks' hell,
or crumpled on your kitchen floor grasping
for something to save you,
or maybe broken on a dirty sidewalk
in some foreign town,
surrounded by dumb
and useless faces -
however it happens, you'll finally
be struck by the perfect
uselessness of it all,
and you'll regret every day wasted
in the service of the dreams of billboards.
As you slip back
to your place in the void,
you'll curse the moment
you bought into the lie of
getting shit done,
and even all the books
and the poems will seem
superfluous.
All you'll wish for
is time enough
for a little more music,
maybe while enjoying
a bottle of something good,
one more day wandering the city

doing nothing in particular,
desperately wondering
if there's some kind of last-second
deal you could make with whomever
is in charge of such matters
that would let you go back
and say that one thing
you'd always
meant.

The Busted Neon Loneliness

I'm drinking wine from a box in a Tenderloin joint
that's all empty flash and hipster art strewn
about steampunk walls.
I've run out of poems
and pretty things to say,
I've got nothing left with which
to poster paint the void,
no defense against the day
other than to get drunk and walk
the downtown streets
with the suicides and pretty girls
as ash from distant fires drifts
down like snow,
blanketing the busted neon loneliness
of massage parlors and lotto machines.
There's a man on a stretcher on Post Street
gasping for air with his dirty belly hanging out
and in Chinatown old men sit on crates
smoking outside the butcher shops,
staring through the muddy years.
I breathe it all in like a sick perfume.
The beautiful terror of it
is the answer to everything,
and it makes me ashamed
for every time I ever asked for anything,
every time I thought to taint the hours
with dreams of purpose.
I just want to dissolve into the laughter
of the televisions in the corner bars
and the smoke from the cigarettes held just so

in the skinny fingers of the girls huddled
outside the gentleman's clubs
and just drift with the ghosts of the forgotten poets
and the crazies and the long dead bartenders,
embracing the terrible music of it,
becoming a golden bright nothing
caught in the amber of the day
like an empty god drunk
on the fire of everything.

Margaritaville

You're in New Orleans in the French Quarter,
hungover on a balcony at 10 a.m.
drinking a champagne cocktail from a plastic cup.
You've just ordered crawfish etouffee
even though you can't remember what etouffee is.
In some tourist trap across the street
a local band plays Margaritaville
and for the first time in your life, you think, hey
that's a pretty good song,
all the while blissfully unaware that hours from now
you'll be mugged on Burgundy St.
staggering back to your room.
So when the man asks you, you say what the hell
and order another plastic cup of champagne,
gazing down on all the women
floating along Bourbon Street with their flowery dresses
drinking neon colored drinks
with fat straws in cups the size of fish bowls,
all of them laughing like death will never be a thing
and you haven't the strength to argue.

William Taylor Jr. lives and writes in the Tenderloin neighborhood of San Francisco. His work has been published widely in journals across the globe, including Rattle, The New York Quarterly, The American Journal of Poetry, and The Chiron Review. He is the author of numerous books of poetry, and a collection of short fiction. He is a Pushcart Prize nominee and was a recipient of the 2013 Kathy Acker Award. He edited *Cockymoon: Selected Poems of Jack Micheline*, published by Zeitgeist Press in 2017.